THE JAMIL COMMENTARIES

60th Anniversary Commemorative Edition

A Companion Volume to
Jamil: Child of Light, Messenger of God
Compiled by Gene Savoy Jr.

THE SACRED TEACHINGS OF LIGHT
CODEX 1

THE JAMIL COMMENTARIES

60th Anniversary Commemorative Edition

A Companion Volume to
Jamil: Child of Light, Messenger of God
Compiled by Gene Savoy Jr.

JAMILIAN UNIVERSITY PRESS

Full use of this volume is subject to oral instruction, taken from the Sacred College of the Jamilian University of the Ordained of the International Community of Christ, 643 Ralston Street, Reno, Nevada, 89503, by its authorized and licensed teachers, ordained and under pastorship papers.

First Edition Copyright © 1973
ICC/International Community of Cosolargy

Copyright © 2022 The Head Overseer (Bishop)
of the International Community of Christ,
Church of the Second Advent,
and His Successor, a Corporation Sole.

PAPERBACK ISBN 978-1-949360-11-0
EBOOK ISBN 978-1-949360-10-3

All Rights Reserved. Copyright fuels creativity, encourages diverse voices, promotes free speech, and creates a vibrant culture. Thank you for buying an authorized edition of this book and for complying with copyright laws by not reproducing, scanning, or distributing any part of it in any form without permission.

PRINTING HISTORY

First Edition 1973
Second Edition 2022

Published by the Jamilian University Press

Religion / Spirituality

FOREWORD

by Gene Savoy, Jr.

The wolf shall live with the lamb, the leopard shall lie down with the kid, the calf and the young lion and the fatling together, and a little child shall lead them.
—Isaiah 11:6

THIS COMPANION VOLUME to *Jamil: Child of Light – Messenger of God* was originally compiled in 1973, the same year the main manuscript was published. Now, on the 60th anniversary of Jamil's passing and after a lapse of forty-nine years, we are again pleased to offer this series of six moving and inspirational impressions of this miraculous Child of Light from individuals who knew, met, and personally experienced him. Together with this foreword, and his natal chart compiled by the esteemed astrologer and mystic Myra Kingsley, these commentaries serve to convey the living story of Jamil.

Jamil was an actual person who lived, taught and passed out of our world in 1962 high in the Callejón de Huaylas near Peru's highest peak, Huascarán. The book *Jamil: Child of Light – Messenger of God* recounts his remarkable life and is one of the most intriguing and unusual books ever written. A true story and deeply moving, it describes the short life of a most remarkable and extraordinary personage – a wondrous and esteemed Emissary of Light who, from a spiritual point of view, can be compared to The Buddha and Jesus Christ.

I had the privilege of knowing everyone associated with these commentaries. As a boy, I met and knew them all, including the astrologer Myra Kingsley, who also compiled my natal chart. (I was also privileged to have met in 1984 Oscar Egusquiza, referred to as "the hunchback" in the book Jamil.) And, perhaps it goes without saying, Jamil's natural father was also mine.

The people who wrote these inspirational commentaries were people not unlike you and me. They were seekers of universal truths, sensitives and mystics, and they yearned for spiritual enlightenment. In their own words, you will read how Jamil was surrounded by rays of light emanating from out of his eyes – the light encompassing his whole being. You will read how he sometimes communicated wordlessly from his deep blue eyes. And you will read the impressions Jamil left on those who received and experienced his very special presence.

The astrologer Myra Kingsley was one of these interesting people and one of the most prestigious astrologers of the 20th century. In 1938, LIFE Magazine described her as "the world's best known astrologer," and many famous people beat a path to her door, including the mystics Edgar Cayce, Eileen Garrett, Manly P. Hall, and Herewood Carrington. In 1926, she met Dr. Annie Besant, the president of the Theosophical Society, Charles Leadbetter, and Jiddu Krishnamurti in

Ommen, Holland. Leadbetter and others espoused the belief that the Society's main purpose was to prepare humanity for the future reception of a "torch-bearer of Truth" – an emissary from spiritual realms who was identified by the Theosophists as the "World Teacher."

As a Theosophist, Myra became familiar with the concept of the coming spiritual emissary – the prophesied Lord Maitreya or Lord of Truth foretold in ancient Buddhist and Jain scriptures. While the Society believed that Krishnamurti himself was what they called "The Coming," he repudiated that concept and in 1934 dissolved the Order of the Star in the East which had been built around him. In 1940, Myra met with Krishnamurti at his home in Ojai, California, and they were both convinced that the coming of the world teacher – the Lord Maitreya – was imminent.

The word Maitreya means "Compassionate One" in both Sanskrit and Pali. In Buddhist eschatology, Maitreya is the future Buddha, the embodiment of Loving Kindness and True Friendship – the spiritual successor to Siddartha Gautama, the Sakyamuni Buddha. He was prophesied to appear on earth in an age when dharma or "The Way" will have been largely forgotten and the world will be in a spiritual void. It was written that he will come to earth from his heavenly abode as a miraculous human child and restore the pure dharma. Unlike his antecedent, he was to be composed more of light than of matter. His coming was to be marked by a number of physical and celestial events, and his arrival was to signify the end of an age characterized as a low point in human moral and spiritual existence. In addition to his role as an Emissary of God, Maitreya is also styled as a chakravarti. (For more on this identification, I refer the reader to the preface of *Jamil: Child of Light*.)

The Child, Jamil, was and is a universal figure. As a Being of Light, he resides in Worlds of Light and is as much alive now as he ever was on Earth. It is foolish to think that children cannot be inspired of God: Look to the scriptures, and recall the prophecies made by the three shepherd children at Fatima, Portugal in 1917 and the Miracle of the Sun that transpired on that auspicious day.

Jamil left the human family with a profound spiritual legacy. Following his passing, he founded a Holy Order and living Community of disciples, the instrument of Christ on earth dedicated to preserving the Sacred Teachings of Light. This is the Community which my father built and which I now have the privilege of serving as head bishop and first successor.

My hope in writing this foreword to the 60th anniversary commemorative edition is to encourage you to write down your own impressions of Jamil if you have experienced or sensed his presence. I know they will be profound.

Gene Savoy, Jr.
February 2, 2022
Reno, Nevada

Gene Savoy, Jr. is the eldest son of the late Gene Savoy, Sr. ("The Man") and half-brother of Jamil ("The Child"). Born in Mexico City, Gene has been practicing the System of Cosolargy since birth. Dedicated by his father to serving The Light atop the Pyramid of the Sun at Teotihuacán, Mexico and later also baptized by him in the waters of the Pacific Ocean off Acapulco, Gene is dedicated to leading the new global spiritual movement based on the Universal System of Cosolargy, which he directs internationally from Cosolargy headquarters in Reno, Nevada, USA.

Educated his entire life in the Sacred Teachings of Light and Cosolargy, Gene succeeded his father as President of Cosolargy International and Head Bishop-Overseer of the International Community of Christ, Church of the Second Advent, upon his father's passing on September 11, 2007. In that capacity, he also serves as President of the Jamilian University of the Ordained, from which he graduated with various degrees.

Widely traveled, Gene regularly visits and presides at venues worldwide on behalf of Cosolargy International and the Jamilian University bringing people together and introducing them to the Sacred Teachings of Light. Gene has traveled extensively expanding Cosolargy International and its teachings to Japan and Mexico. He is currently seeking to do the same in Peru, Australia and New Zealand, Canada, Europe, and Africa. His expertise and skills as an effective communicator, team builder, creative planner and speaker, along with his fundraising and outreach abilities, propel his visionary outlook for the future.

An avid reader and student of history, theology, and metaphysics, Gene is author of *Solar Teachings Greece and the Mediterranean*, a textbook in comparative studies used in the curriculum of the Academy for the Study of the Religious Arts, Spiritual Sciences and Therapeutic Technologies of Cosolargy. Gene married Radheka Patel in 2012 and is the proud father of six – four daughters, one step-daughter, and a son.

LIST OF ILLUSTRATIONS

All illustrations are property of the International Community of Christ, Church of the Second Advent.

- FRONT COVER: 10"x14" oil and pencil on canvas board. No notes on back.
- Natal chart of Jamil with Myra Kingsley's signature
- Myra Kingsley circa 1968
- 14"x18" oil painting on canvas board by Myoko Koshin circa 1973
- Myoko Koshin (Carolyn Mary Snyder) circa 1973
- 14"x18" oil painting on canvas board. Notes on back: "October 23, 1973,
- The Child, Myoko Koshin, 14"x18", original oil painting"
- James Charles Geoghegan circa 1974
- 8½" x 11" drawing in pencil
- Anne Grischuk circa 1978
- Crop from passport photo of Jamil and Gene Savoy Sr.
- Alexander Chukwuma Nwajei circa 1979
- 8½" x 11" digital image cutout from photograph circa 1962
- Ellen Gertrude Seaman circa 1973
- Passport photo of Gene Savoy Sr. and Jamil circa late 1961 before their trip to Mexico in 1962.
- Paula Lazelle Valberde circa 1962
- Community Members group photo taken in Mexico City on June 23, 1962, when the "Act of Formation of ICC" was adopted twenty weeks after the passing of The Child.
- BACK COVER: 76" x 44" etching and acrylic on steel by Buell Mullen circa 1976–1978

TABLE OF CONTENTS

- 1 • Foreword
- x • List of Illustrations
- 13 • Note from The Editors
- x • The Child: Jamil's Natal Chart
- x • The Man's Chart
- x • The Child: Christ Beckons A Buddhist Nun
- x • A Personal Contact with The Child: Christ
- x • The Child: Christ—Compassion and Joy
- x • The Child: A Unifying Symbol Among the Races
- x • A Mother's Response to the Child: Christ Volume
- x • Interview: Paula Valberde and Gene Savoy, Head Overseer of Cosolargy

At that time the disciples came to Jesus and asked, "Who is the greatest in the kingdom of heaven?" He called a little child , whom he put among them, and said, "Truly I tell you, unless you change and become like children, you will never enter the kingdom of heaven. Whoever becomes humble like this child is the greatest in the kingdom of heaven. Whoever welcomes one such child in my name welcomes me."

– MATTHEW 18:1-5

A person old in days will not hesitate to ask a little child of seven days about the place of life, and the person will live.

– GOSPEL OF THOMAS, LOGION 4

NOTE FROM THE EDITORS

The original text of the commentaries from 1973 has not been edited for inclusion, grammatical convention, or general readability. The words of the commentators remain as they were written by them at that time. However, wherever possible, the biographical notes on the commentators have been revised to bring them up to date. The images of Jamil, photographs of the commentators, and the group photo that appear in this volume did not appear in the original publication; they have been added for the record and to enhance the beauty of the volume.

The book JAMIL: CHILD OF LIGHT – MESSENGER OF GOD originally appeared in 1973 under the title JAMIL: THE CHILD CHRIST, and that is how the book is referenced by the commentators in this volume, whose comments were recorded in that year.

Contemporary readers may balk at the commentators' use of the terms *man* and *mankind*, and so it may be useful to explain the use of these terms.

In the effort to render the English language gender-neutral in recent years, the words "human" and "humankind" are commonly and unthinkingly used to replace the words "man" and "mankind" because the word "man" in modern times is often used in a restricted sense to refer exclusively to males.

However, this narrowing of the meaning of man reflects a constriction of overall human thought. The word *man* – like Russian **chelovek** and German *Mensch* even today – originally designated all humanity, both men and women, *as thinking, intelligent beings.*

The Latin word *humanus*, from which we get our modern human, came into Latin completely separate from humus, meaning the organic constituent of soil, but the two terms are related. Along with the term *homo*, used in the designation of our species *Homo sapiens*, these words come from a form of the Proto-Indo-European word **(dh)ghomon-*, whose literal meaning is close to "earthling" or "being of the earth," earth here referring directly to dirt or soil. This association of humankind as a "being of earth" is widespread. Even the biblical story of the origins of humankind has life being breathed into a pile of dust. It is no coincidence that the first human is named Adam, from the Hebrew *adamah*, meaning ground.

As you will learn in this book, ancient prophets and philosophers taught that *Man* was made in the Image of God, not as a physical being, for the physical body was related to the lesser nature of man, but as a Light body made in the image of the greater Light of God. This Light body was the archetype of Man – the true nature – from which evolved the physical form through some fault or transgression against God.

So while some readers might take exception to the use of the word man on the grounds that, at least in today's usage, it seems to exclude half the total number of sentient, thinking beings on the planet, we have decided to continue to use the original meaning of the English word, whose usage has been constricted and corrupted over the past ten centuries.

Hence in all our publications we continue to use the term *Man* with a capital *M*, not only in an effort to retain the association of the term with a divine as opposed to a material, earthly origin, but also to draw upon the original, uncorrupted meaning of the word man as a manifestation of "eternal Mind." For this reason, whenever you see *Man* with a capital *M*, know that this includes you.

THE CHILD
Jamil's Natal Chart

The child was born on Monday, March 16, 1959 at 8:52 A.M. in New Smyrna Beach, Florida. Lat. 29° N. Long. 80° W.

In the book, page 43, his birth-hour is mentioned as "Daybreak" but this is not entirely correct. The sun is not very high in the heavens at 8:52 A.M., but it is not, technically speaking, "daybreak." And if Jamil had been born at daybreak or sunrise it would not have given him as strong and comprehensive a chart as this after-sunrise chart provided—as you will presently see.

Two very important factors are immediately revealed—that Jamil was born within 24 hours of his own mother's birthday ... (March 15th) ... and that the hour of his arrival (8:52 A.M.) brought the 19th-degree of Taurus rising on the ascendent of his chart—which is the exact degree of the sun in his father's chart ... father's birthday May 11th ... and could be the only hour and minute in the whole 24-hours of March 16th, 1959 when the exact degree was on the ascendant of Jamil's natal chart.

So his father's Sun illuminated Jamil's personality and brought radiance to his bodily form, as is described so often in the pages of the book. The mother's Sun was very close, very warm ... in fact a very happy Sun at the time Jamil was born ... yet the mother's Sun's brightness diminished in the course of time, perhaps especially during Jamil's last days. That hour of his passing was at midnight—the Sun at the lowest point in the chart, the "nadir."

With 19° -Taurus rising there is great emphasis in Jamil's chart on his friendly and poetic nature—that he was a "friend to all the world" and it seems that even wild creatures recognized this and were always attracted to him and were never disposed to do him harm. Humanitarianism and charity and sympathy are expressed in Jamil's ruling planet Neptune in the sixth-house of his chart; brotherhood-of-man and philanthropic motives in his seventh-house Jupiter...attributes which, of course, would have come to full fruition if he had lived to manhood. The close proximity of Venus and Mercury in the 12th-house indicates his devotion to beauty and harmony ... Mercury forms words and Venus is. He had a life of travel which is shown with Uranus in the 4th-house of his chart. The home-location changed often ... Uranus moves.

All the signs of the Zodiac belong to the elements of Earth, Air, Fire and Water. Pisces, a "water-sign," may have been significant in Jamil's water-poisoning. Taurus, a "earth-sign," could have placed him amid the ruins of the city of Yungay ... but these are speculative statements and we leave question-marks after them. Nevertheless, if an experienced Astrologer had been given Jamil's date-of-birth and asked to read the chart without knowledge of his, Jamil's, sublime heritage, the Astrologer would have been immediately impressed by the strong and purposeful character of this person—the sense of integrity and honor—the broad-minded vision—the friendliness—the poetic approach of an artist, a materialistic, nor what the Bible calls a "sluggard." The favorable elements were deepened and intensified. The unfavorable were minimized. The father-influence was overall.

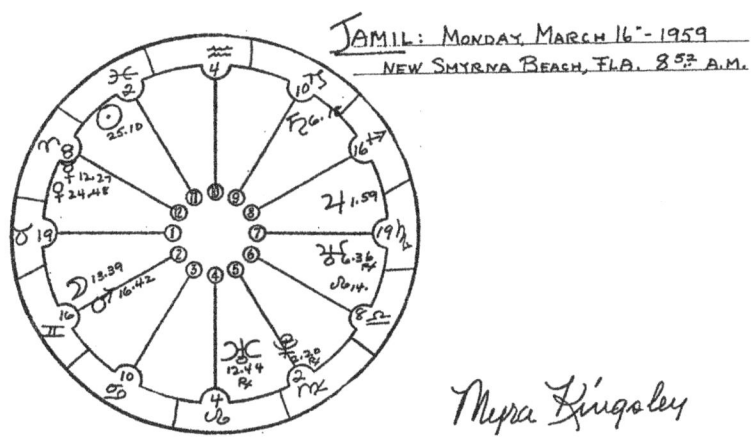

THE MAN'S* CHART

June 1948: "Returned to the world" ... But afflictions to the Moon in The Man's chart at that time suggest suffering connected with the break in leaving his earlier religious teachers and teaching.

August 14, 1955: On that date five planets conjoined with the Sun in the sign of Leo, very close to the position of Neptune in The Man's chart. Neptune is the planet associated with visions and/or spiritual inspiration.

January 21, 1956: This could have been a date of Cosmic significance and may have originated planetary aspects which can verify many of the things that have guided The Man into the word he is now doing.

April 14, 1957: Arrival in Peru. This was the date of the Full-Moon of that month. A "completion" can occur at the time of the Full-Moon. Perhaps that he felt his journey was ended in Peru.

October 21, 1957: The experiences of this date are "beyond Astrology" ... Almost impossible to interpret planetarily.

Submitted by Myra Kingsley, Astrologer
October 23, 1973

MYRA KINGSLEY was born in Westport, Connecticut, in 1897. She graduated from the Juilliard School of Music, where she studied singing, composition, and music theory. Between 1924 and 1927 she performed in the Eastman's School of Music Opera Company in Rochester, New York. Later she met Evangeline Adams who encouraged her to take up a career in Astrology, which she did after moving to San Francisco and studying with Milton Pierce Throop. Following a European tour where she participated in Krishnamurti's seminars, she returned to New York to practice Astrology. Less than a decade later, *Life Magazine* called her the world's best known Astrologer (1938).

A true seeker after truth, Myra came into contact with Gene Savoy, Sr. and began her studies in the school of Cosolargy in 1967. In a letter dated January 31, 1970, she wrote to him saying:

> *... no longer need I consider astrology as the ultimate answer to every problem. I realized that whatever powers I had as an astrologer came through the workings of a higher set of laws than planetary ones. So, as you know, dear Gene, I have been seeking out those more comprehensive channels of spiritual life and being ever since.... The sequence of events and happenings that led me*

from those long-ago amateurish beginnings to what I must recognize now, today, as the proper place for my astrological work and my more advanced spiritual development.

She was a visitor to our headquarters in Peru in 1969 and 1970, in Mexico in 1971, and in Reno in 1974. She passed away on November 20, 1996 at the age of 99 years. Myra did the natal chart not only for Jamil but also for Gene Savoy, Sr. and Jr.

* Gene Savoy, Sr., one of the principal persons in the story told in the book Jamil: Child of Light – Messenger of God and the book's author, is referred to as "The Man" here in the natal chart just as he is in the book.

THE CHILD
Christ Beckons a Buddhist Nun

My first contact with the Worlds of Light burst upon me without the slightest warning or apparent reason many years ago. The day had been of the usual meaningless—dreary sort—holding no intimation of any possible improvement in the future. Dejectedly I prepared for sleep when, just as I began to slip under the covers of my bed, the pitch-black room was suddenly flooded with the most brilliant light I had ever seen; the midday sun at its brightest paled before it, yet it was pleasant and soothing to the eyes.

At the foot of the bed stood a majestic Being of Light with whom I felt at one while still remaining definitely myself. He communicated wordlessly with me in symbols, indescribable forms seen from inside and outside simultaneously, and colors of hue and subtlety inaccessible to the human physical eye. I was being lifted into another Dimension—a Dimension of Light, Beauty, Meaning and Purpose; of Love, Compassion and Joy—all in their essence.

Although 25 years of age, I was alive for the first time! I knew and believed then that God had some purpose for me and I chose to follow this star for the rest of my life regardless of where it might lead. Without knowing why, I thought "This must be Christ." Then followed long periods of search for understanding, for ways to make permanent this expanded awareness, appreciation and communication. Above all, I longed to live every moment of the day in the Light of this Christ Presence—to love, adore and serve. But I didn't know how. This passion for truth went beyond my own Church. I devoured mystical books, tried one path after another. This search; this reading, thinking, mystical practices were of great help in molding, shaping and refining my character; they made me more tolerant, more understanding of human weakness, more compassionate and empathetic—but they seemed to bring me not one inch closer to The Presence. In fact, my tremendous experience had faded to a beautiful memory which drew and tantalized me ever onward.

Years passed. I was widowed; my children grew up and married, and it was necessary to support myself. While I never forgot my main purpose in life, it did get pushed to the background while I was devoting my energies toward preparing myself for the business world. Then I experienced a strange dream. I saw myself as a young woman flying about her work and leaving her baby neglected and dormant in his crib for years without food, water, or care. He was still alive, but just barely. When I awoke I knew what the dream meant: the Presence was still calling me; the child of the dream was my own neglected spiritual self. And so I intensified my search, entering into a school of Yoga which gave me more control over my mind and body, but somehow failed to fill my spiritual needs. Then a beloved relative began urging me to join him in a system I had never encountered before—Cosolargy. To please him, I enrolled as a student and soon found that this was the help I had sought—the teachings struck a responsive chord and the techniques gradually opened me to the World of Light.

Since the headquarters of Cosolargy were at that period of time located in Peru, it was necessary for me to practice alone. Thinking to train myself in meditation so that I would be more sensitive to these higher influences, I undertook a study in the system of Buddhism. As time went by I entered a Buddhist Monastery and became a Nun. There, under the severe discipline required, my many thoughts quieted down and I was able to practice the techniques of Cosolargy with more intensity during many of the long hours of meditation. The result was a gradual expansion of consciousness and periods of renewed contact with the Christ Presence. I told my Buddhist Master some of my experiences—and especially the first and most intense one which he said was an experience of Kensho (enlightenment) and should NOT be talked about to scoffers. He implied that I must keep it to myself so as not to become proud or egotistical as Kensho is what Buddhists aim toward as their goal.

Then Cosolargy moved to the United States and I was impelled both from within and from without to become ever more active in the work. This I was glad to do—spiritually—and as long as I could stay in the Monastery to which I felt obligated. But apparently more was required of me; I resisted with all my strength, rationalizing every sign I received, every leading which came, to make them conform with my determination to stay where I felt I was needed.

On June 21, 1972, at about 5:00 p.m., as I was meditating in the Monastery, the Presence again came to me with great intensity—but in a somewhat different manner than the first time. Before my eyes appeared a beautiful Golden Child. I was aware only of his head in a fiery whirling Sunwheel of flashing changing colors, and particularly of his magnetic eyes which held me spellbound as the iris of each eye whirled about the pupils and changed from blue to silver and to gold, drawing my whole being into them and through them into the Sun and the World of Light. I was in a higher dimension of Being, in a Center of Love, of Energy, of Wisdom. He conveyed to me that I must become wide open to His leadings so that The Light could pour through me to help illuminate my fellow men. This made me very happy and I told myself, "I can do this right here in the Monastery without going out into the world." From that time on it seemed that practically every dream and every vision I had—even every thought—ended up with my seeing the Child in the Sunwheel. Even a trip to Japan for many weeks did nothing to diminish His influence. Since it was just about the time that many had predicted the arrival of Maitreya Buddha, I accepted this Child of Light as the Expected One.

When I was asked to make sketches for the forthcoming book THE CHILD:CHRIST I joyously agreed. When I opened the envelope containing the photo of Jamil from which I was to make the sketch, I gasped with amazement. There was my Child: Christ of the Sun wheel! Then and there I knew that Cosolargy must come first—but I was torn by fear of the possibility of leaving the people who had done so much for me even though I knew it was my destiny to "follow the star." I decided to offer all my free time to work for Cosolargy from the Monastery and prepared myself to do this. Again the Child came to me, this time in a dream that embraced my waking state. He gave me verbal instructions in a beautiful voice which sounded like music. He left no doubt in my mind that I must go West where I was most needed. But how to do this? Was I being unfair, self-centered in following these leadings? I knew by past experience that if I was open to guidance and really trusted and put myself in the hands of the Presence, He would open the way for me.

So, to be sure I was not deceiving myself by following my own desires, I put it all in His Hands and went on as usual. I knew that if I were really meant to leave I would be given an unmistakable sign—I waited. It was not long in coming. Shortly following this decision I had a breakdown in health which made it impossible to continue the severe monastic discipline and, after a period of rest and complete recovery of health with my family, I came to the Center to dedicate my entire being to the joy of helping spread The Light.

I am convinced that The Child: Christ is also The Child: Buddha, as well as the Maitreya Buddha and many others: all in one. Just as there is only ONE SUN shining upon this earth, so is there only ONE PRESENCE, or GOD, or INTELLIGENCE, or SPIRIT, or whatever other term one might care to use.

I will always remain a dedicated Nun; I still combine meditation with the Cosolargy techniques; I still check my spiritual progress with my Master. The greatest change is that my Master is now The Child: Christ, the Leading Sun-Star of my youth and the Companion and Guide of my everyday life.

MYOKO KOSHIN (Carolyn Mary Snyder) was born in Toledo, Ohio, in 1903. She attended the University of Toledo, where she majored in English; she also trained at Davis Business College. She studied economics at the University of Defiance, and law, languages and art at various other institutions. Widowed, she became a legal secretary; she worked for Guideposts Magazine published by Norman Vincent Peale. Her interest in Cosolargy began in 1960. She studied Buddhism for five years and became an ordained Nun in 1972 at age 69. In 1973, following a Vision of The Child, Jamil, she became attached to the International Oversee of Cosolargy in Reno, Nevada. She passed away in 1996.

A PERSONAL CONTACT WITH THE CHILD: CHRIST

It was during the summer of 1960 that I first saw The Child Jamil. I was on a rooftop in Xalapa—City of Flowers—in Mexico, when he came to me, floating over the floor as he did, like a bubble, drifting along yet walking upright with great dignity. I hadn't been told anything about the infant—he could not have been much more than two years of age at the time—and his appearance as if from out-of-nowhere startled me. I thought, at first, he was an optical illusion brought on by the bright morning sun. I had been laying there, absorbing the rays of the sun and reflecting on the earlier forms of solar religions among the peoples of the British Isles, the Persians, Egyptians, Indians and the Pre-Inca and Mayas of America; the continuity of it and the modern form known to the world as Cosolargy. In fact, I had traveled to Mexico to learn directly from Gene Savoy.

Suddenly, a mere babe started talking to me about my very thoughts: "I am Jamil, and I see you are interested in the sun's energy." I rose up nodding to this amazing figure who radiated a light about him like the image of the sun itself. He proceeded to speak to me of the flow of energy from the solar system to man's mind/body. All this from a two-year old! It crossed my mind The Child may have been parroting the words of other adults either being trained in or teaching the system. Infants do not ordinarily speak such wise words. But then, I began to see that he had not captured the words of anyone. He was, in fact, reading my mind. It was startling, to say the least.

We talked, and he mentally communed with me telling of the possibility of a spiritual regeneration of our planet and all its inhabitants. His eyes shone with rayed light and his aura was Golden Light. Then he moved away still radiating energy, leaving me with my thoughts. I was so flabbergasted that I just lay back down to contemplate the actual weight of his thoughts, which he had directed to me by speech and mental projection. I shall never forget how he looked as he glided away, scintillating—radiating light and purity of being and purpose. He was, as it seemed to me, blessing me with this contact. I shall never forget how he looked then. In my meditations I can see Him to this day with His hands raised in benediction.

Lest the reader accuses me of fuzzy thinking, it seems proper at this time to write briefly of my background. I was born in Ireland where I studied and grew up interested in Philosophy, Science and the Humanities. I was a total Agnostic at age 19 even though I was brought up in the arms of the Church and it was, at one time, thought by my wonderful mother that I might have the makings of a Priest. However, I became disillusioned with the secular structure of the Church and the trend of Christianity. Wonderfully honest and dedicated men are involved in the Churches, but the orientation involved seemed to me to be wrong—they were losing their real reason for existence by becoming social structures instead of religious.

Dr. Carl Jung and Dr. Victor Frankel are two persons in the modern Psychological movement who seem to have some of the answers: man is basically a religious being and the only way to true happiness lies in this direction.

I studied the various religions and schools of Psychology; their philosophies and psychologies—Hinduism, Yoga, Vedante, Buddhism, Zen included; Sufi ideas, magic, witchcraft and Druidism. I studied Prof. William James, McDougall, Pavlov, Watson, Ouspensky, Gurdjieff and Nicoll. My belief in religion was restored, purified and made whole: The world's great religions had all been created for the purpose of raising man's level of God Consciousness, but through time had lost their original direction and savour. "Except ye become as little children ye cannot enter the Kingdom of Heaven." So spoke Jesus to the learned and so-called wise scribes and pharisees. He knew that intellect alone with its fracturization and its labeling complex destroys inner truth and growth. Whole schools of Philosophy follow this trend of labeling ideas, calling this knowledge. The attainment of wisdom can never, or almost never, be arrived at by labeling and fragmentation processes. Intuition, meditation, contemplation are the beginning of knowledge and wisdom. Even pragmatic science will admit that most inventions and creative ideas were obtained after the seeker had let go of the intellectual process and allowed the intuitive center to take over. Answers came from nowhere in a flash, like those of a child when the spirit shines through.

During 30 years of study and travel over the United States, Canada, Europe, Australia, New Zealand and North Africa, I have observed that man has become disillusioned. Religion, Philosophy, Psychology and the physical sciences have combined to bring about such fragmentation of the mind/body and Spirit that it parallels the breakdown of the Roman Empire and the early advent of Christianity. At that time there was an overabundance of mystic cults—as there is today. The reason for all this is simple. Man is structured for spiritual growth. During periods when morality on all levels has reached the nadir, he becomes desperate in his search for some eternal meaning, and so, is a prime target for the occult arts which continue to fracture man's makeup even further. The result is chaotic.

It would seem to me that when the Heart of Divine Solar Consciousness sends forth a ray to correct this condition, it comes through in the aspect of The Child idea, showing a way of love, as came to ancient peoples. Krishna came to Hinduism at its time of travail in the same manner: and by love conquered.

Jesus appeared at the epitome of Jewish and Roman legalism. He came to show a way to Heaven through the re-creation of the untarnished consciousness of the Childlike state. And to show that the decline of legalism "an eye for an eye and a tooth for a tooth" was not the answer to man's problems; he taught forgiveness.

The Tower of Babel is the supreme example of man's intellectual arrogance to reach Heaven by material powers: an impossible task. Again the admonition of Jesus: "Except ye become as a little child...."

The reason for the above thesis on the childlike state was brought about by my contemplation of the short visit of Jamil with me, there on the roof in Xalapa, Mexico many years ago. He has been in my thoughts and dreams so much these past years, and the book on The Child:Christ which is a source of inspiration to anyone who reads it, confirmed my secret idea that He was indeed a Messenger from the Source of All. Looking back now, I remember how He seemed such a small angel and yet spoke with the wisdom of the ages. This fact has caused me much soul-searching thought over the years and I am very glad that I had the brief opportunity of meeting with Him. Actually, since that time I have meditated many times and He floats, as it were, into the meditation always with a Golden Light surrounding Him—"Clothed with the Sun."

With the possibility of being labeled an Emanationist, I keep thinking of the Solar Logos idea more and more; of the possibility of our earth sphere, with all humanity, being radiated and raised upward in Consciousness by the shining forth of Light Energies.

"And A Little Child Shall Lead Them" is the theme which shall be our motto because God has deigned to show Himself through a Child once again in order to inspire a New Dispensation of Christianity. It will be up to us to instill the Faith which we have ourselves in this Modern Miracle. There is a tremendous emotional appeal in the Idea of the Child as Inspirer to Humility as against modern godless materialism which removes from man any idea of Dignity or Humanity, or Humility which is a missing ingredient in our modern society. "Of such is the Kingdom of Heaven" so said Jesus to his Apostles who had misunderstood Him more than they had ever comprehended His Teaching. You can also remember the story of Augustine talking to the Child at the shores of the Mediterranean about comprehending the Wonders of God. If you search you will find that the Christ Child has never left Humanity's side, but no one has listened to His Directions. Remember the Infant of Prague. There is much to be learned from those visitations.

With the new upheaval which is occurring all over the world in the Religious Field, and the destruction of old and dead forms of these said Religions there is a tremendous need for a Revelation which is, as the young say, "for real." We have in Cosolargy such a Revelation with a TRANSFORMING GRACE which is sorely needed in this troubled age of Searching Youth and Materialistic Parents. The tragedy of all this is that Man has made a God of the Theory of Science with sheeplike attitude, and risks the loss of Divine Truth and Good.

I am thankful that Humanity has been blessed once again with the Appearance of the Child, and that His Revelation is available through the Christology of Cosolargy.

Submitted by J. Charles Geoghegan, Lecturer
October 28, 1973

J. CHARLES GEOGHEGAN was born in Aughacashel, Carrick On-Shannon, Leitrim, Ireland in 1922. He was a graduate of the Presentation Brothers College, where he majored in philosophy. Originally he considered a religious vocation but finally elected to pursue philosophy and eastern religion. He studied in England under Maurice Nicoll, a student of Carl Jung, P.D., Ouspensky, and G.J. Gurdjieff, and undertook a career in psychological medicine. With Ouspensky's authorization, he established many study groups.

In 1958, Mr. Geoghegan became interested in Cosolargy while it was a small, isolated school in the Peruvian Andes. Since that time he was a constant contributor and researcher. He received first-level ordination in 1962 and was confirmed to the Sacred Oversee in 1975. In the 1970s, he was engaged as a lecturer, and taught Mantra Yoga to interested groups, including the Catholic Monks of the Holy Ghost at the Cistersian Monastery in Conyers, Georgia. He was also involved in professional athletics. Also in the 1970s, Mr. Geoghegan wrote commentaries on Cosolargy's Decoded New Testament and The Child:Christ, and a short text on his observations and experiences with the Infant Child Jamil. In the 1990s he became involved in osteopathic work in North Carolina. He passed away in 1998.

THE CHILD: CHRIST COMPASSION AND JOY

First of all I would like to say that it seems to me that I have had three experiences regarding The Child. If I am to start at the beginning then I must go back to the year of 1971 (July 5th). On that day, before going to work, I viewed the sun in the woods. As a result, after reporting to work, I felt a certain freshness. Then suddenly, before 9.30 AM., there was a strong fragrance in the air. It had a blossom-like scent. I was secretly happy; the thought occurred to me that this might be the presence of a High Being. Evelyn, a girl who was working close by, came into my department and asked if I was using perfume. I told her no, but that perhaps someone passing by left a scent in the air. She said no, that it was the strongest next to me. From time to time thereafter I was to catch a whiff of this scent (summertime only). Later, I got a letter from Gene saying that I had a visitation of The Child. I'll never forget that day: as I was holding his letter in my hand on the way home, again there was a distinct lovely fragrance in the air. I was in a daze — too happy for words.

Then in July 1972, approximately around the 19th, I saw the eyes of The Child. Looking at the eyes of The Child in Myōkō's sketch brought back the memory of that experience. On the 23rd, at sunset, I had the glorious experience of seeing a beautiful church cross that appeared white in the sun, just before it went down. Had this something to do with The Child?—the timing was so perfect!

And, in 1973, on July 9th, I had the Vision. Two days before, while viewing the sun through blue filters and thinking of The Child, a thin white cross was seen extended over the sun. My thoughts here had something to do with what my Teacher predicted in Mexico. He said that I would find peace of soul. On this morning I found myself thinking, "I believe." Because didn't Jesus say something about believing?

On July 9th, to begin with, I woke up with a strange feeling. Nothing could shake it off. It felt more like a strange energy coursing through my body — at least that is how it struck me. It persisted throughout the day and got progressively stronger by 4.15 P.M. This was due to the fact that on top of the strange feeling, I got myself involved in work that put me under a strain. The thought of facing the next day (the job was not completed) was too much. So, after work I just flopped on the bed and tried to forget it. I managed to doze off. That's when it all started.

Around 5.30 P.M. a scratch on the door by a little dog I had befriended woke me up. But just before I opened my eyes (and I can't be sure if it was a dream or a scene that appeared in the mind's eye) I became aware of a very beautiful child of approximately two years of age. He was standing so I saw the full figure. At first he appeared rather serious. I couldn't help but notice how shapely his little form was. He was clad in a white outfit with a blue trim. If I remember correctly, the blue trim appeared on the short sleeves. And while I have no distinct memory of it, I somehow got the impression there was also a blue trim on the bottom of his short white pants. I wish I could remember the neckline. And it seems to me he wore white shoes. Then instantly I became aware of something alive. What a beautiful Child. He had platinum-like blond, wavy hair of medium length, white flawless skin and beautiful large light blue eyes that seemed to dominate the whole scene. The eyes gazed at me ever so tenderly; there seemed to be joy in them. After gazing at me he turned and as he turned he smiled. Yet, I had the feeling that he came out of great compassion, as though He knew what I was going through. (I indeed was going through a strange period — it reached an all-time high in August and tapered off by the latter part of September.)

Later, in retrospect, I wondered if The Child knew what was to come, because of the way He smiled at the end of the vision as He turned. I use the word "smile" — actually the lips turned up on one side (yet it was a smile of a sort). As He did so He had a look that is hard to describe. I believe I can safely say it was one of compassion. I felt much joy after seeing Him — later, even very excited, for the thought did occur to me that this possibly could be The Child.

Who wouldn't get excited at the prospect —what an honor. On July 31st I had some dreams regarding The Child—too enigmatic to relate. However, I can say this: at one point while in a sitting position (there were others) I saw His face, although the features were not distinct because of the Light which enveloped it. I got the impression He was trying to explain something to me. Then immediately following this, another dream appeared consisting only of two large elongated eyes. They were beautiful light blue eyes and looked at an angle. These appeared to be mature eyes—more like those of a young man's. Yet, I had the distinct impression they were The Child's.

Several hours of concentration regarding my experiences with The Child have left me in a pleasant frame of mind, and I find myself wishing I had a little more leisure time to fully enjoy this feeling. I am looking forward to more experiences in regard to The Child, and the Light he brings.

Submitted by A. Grischuk, Cosolargist
October 20th, 1973

ANNE GRISCHUK was born December 15, 1918 in Elbert, West Virginia. She moved to Ohio in 1941, settling in Yellow Springs where she worked and retired from the Antioch Bookplate Co. She enrolled in Cosolargy Class 15 in 1964 while the Headquarters was based in Peru. She became a dedicated researcher, intelligent and expressive. She was a generous benefactor in many areas such as The Ship's Company to assist in the purchase of the Feathered Serpent II – Ship of Light, the Order of the Child – Monk de Jure and the establishment of the Jamilian Handbell Choir. Anne was a supporter, friend, and Consociate member of the Cosolargy Community from 1964 to her passing in 2008.

THE CHILD

A Unifying Symbol Among the Races

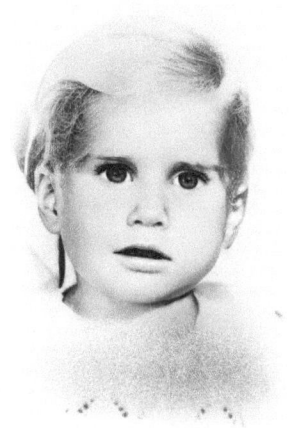

THE CHILD: CHRIST is a living book which appeals to the heart of man and it will always remain one of the most treasured jewels among the world's Sacred Volumes. It announces to the world the appearance of God's greatest Gift to mankind — the Birth of THE CHILD: CHRIST; God made manifest among men.

The Child of Light arrived at a most unique period of the world's history. Science and technology have merged to send man into space and on the moon. It is therefore most appropriate that, in the sphere of Sacred Religion, God has blessed humanity with a Beam of Light, showing the human family that there is a way to Eternal Life with

God. Some think this can be attained externally, through intellectual, scientific and technological achievements: the way is attained internally, by means of the Spirit as taught by High Religion.

The Child: Christ showed humanity the way to God. Most important, he demonstrated the way himself, thus solving the age-old problem of mankind; that which disturbs the mind of every human being: is man immortal? The Child: Christ declared to the world that God has a plan for mankind; that it is by development of individual Christ Consciousness that man achieves Eternal Union with God. He also demonstrated that physical man can achieve this through and within the Universal Christ Force manifest in the Sun of Righteousness, which is available equally to all the nations and races of the world. He revealed the Sun and the Christ-force as the Divine Bread from God and as a Living Force through which man can commune with God and achieve Spiritual Rebirth. He therefore gives a meaning and purpose to Life.

He glorified and unified all the old prophets and Holy men who founded the great world religions, as our Elder Brothers—who held the Office of Christ—and towed that the origin of all these great world religions is from one Divine Source. This Child of the Universe reconciled God and the Spiritual World of Light with the human family of the earthly world.

At a critical moment, when mankind is at the brink of self-destruction through negation, the Holy Child arrives to offer answers to human problems of war, violence and revolution, by teaching mankind the importance of harmonizing and communing with all Living things in Nature; of reflecting the Christ nature to our fellow human beings, animals, plants: to the whole universe. We all have Divine Life in common.

The Child teaches how humanity can bring about the cessation of human misery, sufferings, sin, ignorance, injustice, disease, and other basic ills of the human nature, by righteousness, peace, divine love, inner joy and the better and glorified quality of Life which are the many blessings of a developed Christ Consciousness. He dispels the fears which haunt human minds and the sorrows which surround death of the physical body by stressing the tremendous importance of incarnating the Christ Consciousness which insures immortality of the Soul. He restores the dignity of the human soul and gives a resounding victorious message of great hope and joy.

Therefore, it does not matter in the least what is a man's nationality, race, or religion; whether he calls himself an Englishman, American, Asian, African, Russian, or whatever; it is not important whether he is Muslim, Jewish, Hindu, Christian or Buddhist. The color of his skin, his culture, ethics, intellectual attainments, material wealth, or status in life are all immaterial and unimportant. All man-made inequalities, laws, politics, barriers and limitations can be overcome. They can be transcended by the inner freedom of an enlightened Soul, who lives a truly mystical Life within one's Being; by inwardly radiating the Universal Christ Force. All the diversity may be unified by the common goal of all human beings: the great need to generate the Light Body through the Grace of the Divine Christ manifest in the Sun and available to all equally.

The Child Jamil communicates his message through the Universal Language of Light which registers within each person's consciousness according to his understanding. His teaching and message is to every spiritual aspirant, and to every human being. And, above all, it has practical and daily applications in everybody's life. Its truth is immortal because it holds good for now and for all times as long as human life exists on earth. It has tremendous spiritual impact to awaken and transform the spiritual consciousness of the world for the good of all. The Child: Christ is the Universal One.

This Child of the Universe stresses the importance of harmony and unity, and He prays that God may unify the family of Christ on earth as it is in Heaven.

Submitted by Dr. Alexander Ch. Nwajei, M.D.
October 28th, 1973

ALEXANDER CHUKWUMA NWAJEI was born in Nigeria, in 1939. He graduated from the University of Cairo, Egypt, where he received his degree in medicine. For many years he practiced medicine at the Royal Hospital, Weston-Super-Mare, Somerset, England. Dr. Nwajei began his studies in Cosolargy in 1962, and in 1971 accepted an appointment to head Cosolargy's Medical Research Department. In May of 1981, he returned to his homeland and served as a physician in the Lagos Teaching Hospital in Lagos, Nigeria, where he lived until his death in 2021.

A MOTHER'S RESPONSE TO THE CHILD: CHRIST VOLUME

M y heart is so filled with this beautiful book that I would like to share my response and reactions to it with others.

THE CHILD: CHRIST is the work of a mystical genius, for only under divine inspiration could a book of such magnitude be composed. I fully believe the phrase "mystical genius" is a correct one, for it is said that the mark of a genius is his ability to change the world. And only the mystic can influence the thinking of mankind enough to turn him around to face the Light, thus enabling him to follow the plan of God. Consequently, a book as momentous as this will be felt around the globe, from generation to generation, and beyond. I am sure.

The beginnings of the book flashed into my mind like lightning, revealing a memory I thought long forgotten. I, too, heard the Call from somewhere deep inside. I felt the urge to have a Holy Child. From the years between 1955 and 1959 I was obsessed with the longing for a child from the Angel World, a Child of Light. So, the story of The Child: Christ pierced my heart and resurrected anew the old need and longing. In those days I was driven and couldn't seem to rid my mind of the idea. My rational mind ridiculed such a possibility, but still the idea persisted. At the beginning of 1956 my dreams were filled with pyramidal forms. They so impelled and influenced me that I took a voracious interest in Egypt (my knowledge at that time did not include Mexico or Peru), devouring one book after another, in search of a clue that would indicate what was happening to me. During 1958 I often felt His presence around me.

I see now that I was just sensitive to the great event that was about to occur. While reading the book, all the needs and cravings became clear and pronounced. I lived every moment of the story with The Man; I felt his tender longings for the Child, that preceded his marriage and union with the Woman. I walked every step of the way, sharing the events, until The Man's love for the Child permeated my being. When the Child was born I became every woman bringing forth, from the strength of her body and the love in her soul, a Miracle—a Holy Child so angelic, so beautific that a new world would be awakened at his coming—a precious being capable of lifting the entire human race, changing it from darkness into Light. No sacrifice could be too great, no love large enough to comprehend this Gift of God.

The entire story so filled me with selfless love that my heart expanded. I became as a vessel unable to contain the emotions invoked. My cup overflowed. I wept day and night for three days All through my reading I had to lay the volume aside from time to time because of its potency. It overwhelmed my soul until I could think of nothing else, and finally caused my complete surrender. I united in spiritual love and joy with the entire event: the people became my people, the Child, my child; The Man and his life became a permanent part of my spiritual being. The beauty and meaning of this story is so far above the physical planes that it opens inner eyes and ears.

THE CHILD: CHRIST should be used for spiritual uplifting in all churches. It contains a spiritual force so potent that people are faced with their own "Moment of Truth," whether they so wish it or not, from the depth of "self-meeting-Self," thereby permanently changing the inner image of what everyone sees himself or herself to be. It is an initiation: a spiritual union with the Godhead which results in the acceptance of the Second Advent and the realization that the second coming of Christ is upon us here and now. The Man guides us by deft and knowing ways until we, too, see the Angels of Light and read in our hearts the message that the office of Christ is to be held by those who are able to generate their eternal Body of Light. These dedicated ones will serve as teachers of the Sacred Teachings of Light, until our world, as we know it, shall disappear and a new World of Light shall be formed.

Our only endeavor should be toward forming our own light bodies and uniting in this effort with other Associates who have formed theirs, so that we might influence the population of the earth to bring all humanity into direct communication with the Godhead.

The book glows and the words become almost too bright for the eyes to read as one experiences the Plan for mankind. It has the magical quality of convincing the reader. One knows that the True Church is beginning under Christ turned into the likeness of a Child. It is not a story: it is LIFE. It lives and is as real as we are. It gives forth, with each reading, new information, new directions previously unseen. It continually teaches new concepts, new guidelines. It is self-revealing and God-revealing, and the information acquired nourishes and sustains us, planting seeds of a new knowledge within our souls. These seeds will in their turn develop into even greater powers, greater worlds in an ever-increasing progression.

I find myself contemplating the meaning of the True Church, and the Sun of Righteousness. It is imminent, vast, lofty; so far-reaching that its light will guide the ages ahead. No orthodox church, no religion, no Saints' teachings could equal the universality of this Book. Truly, it is timely. Our world has long needed a new ontology. It can change our lives, and our children's lives and save the universe from destruction and annihilation.

I am awed by its true meaning and I thank God on bended knee for The Man, The Child and the message conveying to us the Eternal Light of the World.

ELLEN SEAMAN was born in Winner, South Dakota in 1919. After studies at the Los Angeles Art Institute and the New York Institute of Technology she began doing portrait work in oils. Mrs. Seaman became an active member of Cosolargy in January, 1973, after spending a year participating in the San Francisco Community of Cosolargy, an authorized group of Associates conducted by the Right Reverend Gene Savoy, Sr. Mrs. Seaman was engaged in making audio recordings of the Essaei Transcript, S.P.A.N lecture series and in compiling a comprehensive portfolio of dream and vision sketches which was to be included in a book to be published by ICC/COSOLARGY. She passed away March 2005 in Long Beach, California.

INTERVIEW

Paula Valberde and Gene Savoy, Head Overseer of Cosolargy

by The Editors

(Gene Savoy, author of THE CHILD: CHRIST, critically analyzes Paula Valberde's impressions of the infant Jamil, during her visit to Veracruz, Mexico, in 1960, where she observed for the first time the amazing child. Mrs. Valberde was a close student of Paramahansa [Yogananda] and Oriental religions before taking up studies in Cosolargy in 1958. The interview was taped on November 20, 1973, and represents a remarkable record between two major confidants of the Child.)

SAVOY: I would like to ask you about your impressions of Jamil when you first saw him at Veracruz, Mexico, so many years ago.

VALBERDE: I shall never forget the first time I saw him. I heard a knock on the door to my room and when I opened it there stood my friend holding the hand of a small child whose form was golden surrounded by rays of light. My being was filled completely with this light. As I studied him, his eyes met mine and he disappeared physically to become part of the whole scene. Then he appeared again in physical form. My first inclination was to fall down on my knees and worship him, not because one should worship an individual, but because of what he represented.

SAVOY: You studied Eastern Teachings and trained with Paramahansa and knew him personally, didn't you?

VALBERDE: Oh, yes, but Jamil is so far above Paramahansa that there's no comparison—not that Paramahansa hadn't reached a certain degree of spiritual advancement.

SAVOY: What did you see about Jamil that impressed you?

VALBERDE: The eyes, the beautiful golden aura—everything. His whole being impressed me; he was some Great Soul that had incarnated for a short while. It couldn't be denied!

SAVOY: Then you don't see that in most teachers?

VALBERDE: Oh no, they haven't reached that expansion of consciousness.

SAVOY: Was it rather strong?

VALBERDE: It was more than 'rather strong'—it was extremely strong! He was, I repeat, a Great Soul who had incarnated, he had come for a purpose and when his purpose was fulfilled, why—then he left the world.

SAVOY: Your many years of study with the Paramahansan Group and others gives you the background to say what you did. And I assume you wouldn't compare Jamil to any teacher.

VALBERDE: Oh, he was above them. He wasn't just a teacher. This boy was a Great Being of Light, as mentioned in the book. He was pure and perfect; immaculate; universal.

SAVOY: Why do you think that this Child came at this time?

VALBERDE: He came as a forerunner of what is meant to be, I would say, to assist humanity to become, to fulfill their destiny.

SAVOY: Has he ever appeared to you since he passed into the Light?

VALBERDE: Yes indeed; last Saturday, November 18th, in fact. I was meditating when all of a sudden he appeared close to me, not completely gold as I usually saw him, but in beautiful colors. I noticed only his beautiful golden head, his glowing face and his wonderful whirling eyes which changed from blue to a lovely soft rose and then violet with the golden aura about him. I uttered his name with a feeling of almost stunned disbelief that so wonderful a thing could happen to me. "Is it really you, Jamil," I asked as he faded. Then, in apparent confirmation of my query, he reappeared with such convincing clarity and force that I could no longer question. I was so glad. It really delighted me. I am not a doubter, still, I always want to be sure. His face was glowing. Oh, just beautiful. He did not smile, but he had a pleased expression.

[NOTE: Just as Paula had finished speaking these words there was a loud "clang" bell-like sound as a walnut-sized cut quartz crystal broke loose from its taped position on the hand of a bronze statue resembling the Child which was sitting on the desk; it jumped about five inches in the air and then landed between the speakers, the room becoming charged with energy. *

SAVOY: That is symbolic. Isn't it? It is amazing.

VALBERDE: Oh, I feel it truly affirms everything I have said—that it was a fact.

SAVOY: It certainly is a confirmation. Jamil is appearing to many at this time, But, let's proceed.]

SAVOY: Now, Paula, we both know the answer, but I'd like to hear your own words. Some ask why the Child had to pass on. They wonder why he couldn't have stayed here. What do you think?

VALBERDE: I think the vibrations of the earthly surroundings were too strong for so spiritual a person. The same thing happened to Jesus. He would come into the cities but He had to go back into the purity of the wilderness of the desert. He couldn't stand those vibrations. But though Jamil has gone on to a higher form of authority, he is the sponsor of this work and he will never leave Cosolargy because he revealed it.

SAVOY: I believe that Jamil, like Jesus and other Great Ones, came from the Worlds of Light, like angels.

VALBERDE: Jamil was beyond that, beyond the angels, as was Jesus.

SAVOY: In our own advanced and technical age of sophistication, with almost everyone interested in Metaphysics and Occultism, and everyone doing his own thing—what do you think is the greatest and most important lesson people can learn from this Child?

VALBERDE: I think he came into this world through the Christian religion to fulfill it and lay the Foundations for a true universal religion. At the time there were not enough people who could understand him or why he came. Although he left after a brief span of years, that is not the end of him. He came from the Light Worlds to leave his Light which is even now felt by many people. But most are not yet ready for Him; they must grow.

SAVOY: That's where the Course of Instruction that we have proves valuable. It teaches people how to develop their inner natures so that they can understand the teachings that Jamil brought forth. Now, Paula, how would you compare this Child to, say, Buddha or some other great teacher from your personal viewpoint?

VALBERDE: Well, to me, Jamil is from the Light Worlds and Buddha was a man who had attained. So, of course, Jamil was the greater of the two.

SAVOY: How would you compare Jamil to Jesus?

VALBERDE: Jesus was a great Avatar, too.

SAVOY: One last question. We talked about what people could learn from this Child, who He might have been and who He was. Now, you have searched all your life and you've studied for nearly six decades. What did the Child do for you as a searcher having all this knowledge and exposure to Paramahansa and other Eastern teachers?

VALBERDE: He did away with all that I had learned. He was beyond learning. He taught me. There's no comparison; I can't even put it into words.

* This taped interview is on record and in the archives of Cosolargy. It will be made available, upon request, to serious investigators.

PAULA VALBERDE was born in Texas in 1905. She relocated to Nevada, settling in Sparks, Reno's neighboring city, with her husband, Lorenzo Valberde, a railroad engineer from California. Paula enrolled in the first original Cosolargy class formed in Peru in 1957 as student No. 4, along with fellow student, J. Charles Geoghegan.

On June 23, 1962 she became one of the signers of the documents that formed ICC-Cosolargy. The following day she received first level ordination in The Community.

Paula offered great support and encouragement when the school was moved from Peru to Reno, Nevada in 1971-72. On August 30, 1975, she received her second ordination and was confirmed as a member of the Sacred Oversee of The Community and given the title of Right Reverend. She served in this capacity until she retired to private life in 1977. Her last meeting with her Teacher Gene Savoy, Sr. was in September, 1990 at the age of 85. She passed away three years later in 1993.

This Community Members group photo was taken in Mexico City on June 23, 1962, when the "Act of Formation of ICC" was adopted twenty weeks after the passing of The Child. The individuals in the photo are listed alphabetically:

- John Anderson
- Rheo H. Clair
- Donald G. Crook
- James Charles Geoghagen
- Harry D. Goodman
- Albertha L. Logan
- William R. Meinke
- Ivan J. Ortiz
- Elvira Clarke de Savoy
- Gene Savoy Sr.
- John A. Scott
- Douglas Sharon
- James H. Speed
- Paula L. Valberde

www.ingramcontent.com/pod-product-compliance
Lightning Source LLC
Chambersburg PA
CBHW040203100526
44592CB00006B/89